HURRICANES

SEYMOUR · SIMON

HarperCollinsPublishers

PHOTO CREDITS

Permission to use the following photographs is gratefully acknowledged: pages 4–5, 14–15, 16 (middle and bottom), © Jim Reed Photography; pages 6–7, 24–25, Science VU/NOAA; page 9, © Kjell B. Sawduey/Visuals Unlimited; page 10, Science VU/NASA; pages 12–13, 17 (bottom), NOAA/Department of Commerce; page 16 (top), © Marc Epstein/Visuals Unlimited; page 17 (top), © Ken Wagner/Visuals Unlimited; page 18, © Charles W. McRae/Visuals Unlimited; pages 20–21, © Lannis Waters/*The Palm Beach Post*; page 22, © Greg Lovett/*The Palm Beach Post*; page 26, © Nancy P. Alexander/Visuals Unlimited; page 29, © David Lane/Visuals Unlimited; page 30, © Arthur R. Hill/Visuals Unlimited.

Library of Congress Cataloging-in-Publication Data
Simon, Seymour.
Hurricanes / Seymour Simon.— 1st ed.
p.   cm.
Summary: Discusses where and how hurricanes are formed, the destruction caused by legendary storms, and the precautions to take when a hurricane strikes.
ISBN 0-688-16291-6 — ISBN 0-688-16292-4 (lib. bdg.)
1. Hurricanes—Juvenile literature.   [1. Hurricanes.]   I. Title.
QC944.2 .S56   2003   551.55'2—dc21   2002151603

1 2 3 4 5 6 7 8 9 10 ❖ First Edition

This book is for
my wonderful grandkids:
Jeremy, Chloe, Benjamin, and Joel

Hurricanes are huge spinning storms that develop in warm areas around the equator. Hurricanes bring strong winds, heavy rains, storm surges, flooding, and sometimes even tornadoes. Coastal areas and islands are in the most danger during a hurricane, but even inland areas are at risk.

Hurricane season along the East Coast of the United States begins in June and continues until the end of November. The peak hurricane months are August and September. The East Coast averages about five hurricanes a year. Over other parts of the world, hurricanes happen year-round.

The word *hurricane* comes from people who lived in the Tropics in earlier times. The ancient Mayan people of South and Central America called their storm god Hunraken. An evil god of the Taino people of the Caribbean was called Huracan. Hurricanes are not really evil, but they can cause terrible destruction and great loss of life.

Hurricanes are one of three kinds of storms called tropical cyclones. Tropical means that the storms form over the warm waters of the Tropics near the equator. Cyclones are storms spinning around a calm center of low air pressure, which also moves. Cyclones spin counterclockwise in the Northern Hemisphere and clockwise in the Southern Hemisphere.

Tropical depressions are cyclones of clouds and thunderstorms that spin around a central area. They have steady wind speeds of 38 miles per hour or less.

Tropical storms are cyclones of heavy clouds and strong thunderstorms that spin at steady wind speeds of 39 to 73 miles per hour.

Hurricanes are the strongest tropical cyclones. They have steady winds of 74 miles per hour or higher. When these storms form over the North Atlantic, Caribbean Sea, Gulf of Mexico, or the west coast of Mexico, they are called hurricanes. In the North Pacific, these kinds of storms are called typhoons, and in the Indian Ocean they are called cyclones. In Australia, hurricanes are called willy-willies, after the word whirly-whirly.

Hurricanes are the only weather disasters that have been given their own names, such as Andrew, Camille, Floyd, Fran, Hugo, Irene, and Opal. In some ways all hurricanes are alike. But like different people, each hurricane has its own story.

All hurricanes form in the same way. They begin life in the warm, moist atmosphere over tropical ocean waters. First, the atmosphere gathers heat energy through contact with ocean waters that are above eighty degrees Fahrenheit to a depth of about two hundred feet. Next, moisture evaporating from the warm waters enters the atmosphere and begins to power the infant hurricane.

The growing hurricane forms bands of clouds and winds near the ocean surface that spiral air inward. Thunderstorms form, heating the air further and forcing the winds to rise higher into the atmosphere and the spinning to increase. Because of their power, hurricanes can easily last more than a week and may strike Caribbean islands days before whirling north and east into the United States.

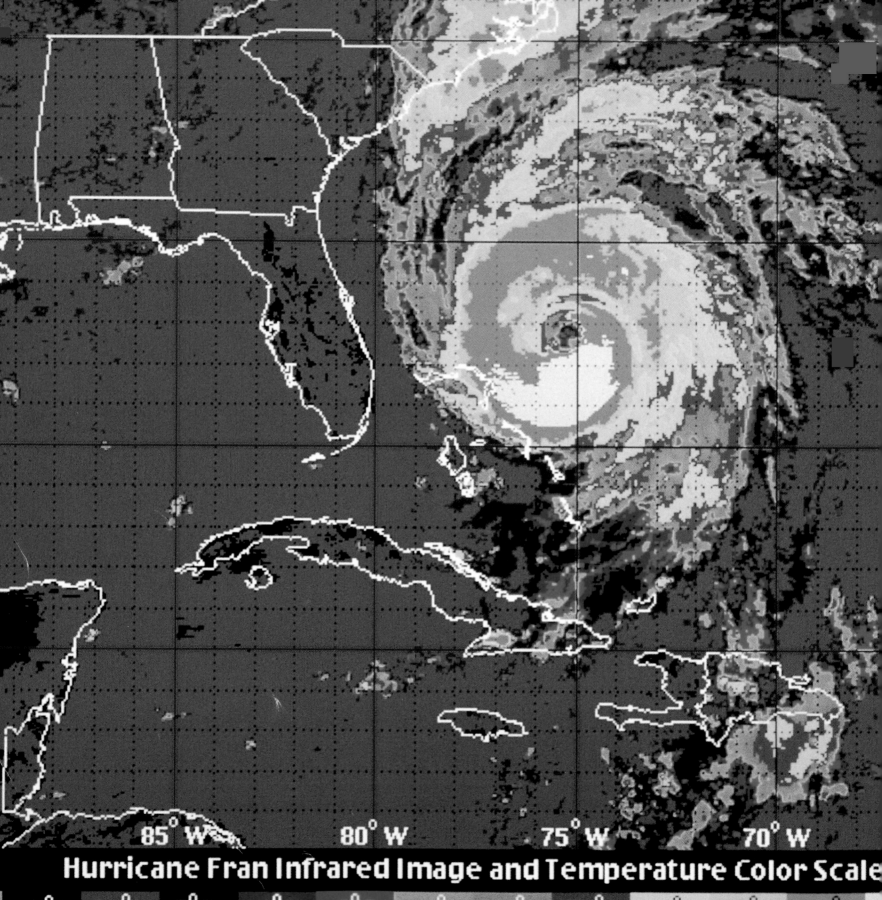

Hurricane Fran Infrared Image and Temperature Color Scale

| >15°C | 15°C | 8°C | -1°C | -6°C | -13°C | -24°C | -34°C | -41°C | -50°C | -57°C |

This satellite photo shows the bands of thunderstorm clouds spiraling in toward its center, or eye. The eye of a hurricane is fairly calm, with light winds and few clouds. But if you are in the eye of a hurricane and you think the worst is over, be warned. The most violent winds and heaviest rains take place in the eye wall, the ring of clouds and thunderstorms closely surrounding the eye. At the top of the eye wall (about fifty thousand feet), most of the air pushes outward and then falls like water from a fountain, but always spinning in a counterclockwise direction in the Northern Hemisphere.

When a hurricane grows to full strength, it can kick up waves fifty feet or higher in open ocean waters. Every second, a large hurricane moves more than a million cubic miles of atmosphere. A typical hurricane can dump from six inches to over a foot of rain across a region.

Hurricane forecasts estimate when the eye will pass over a particular location. But even a small hurricane has damaging winds and rains that may arrive many hours before the eye.

storm surge is a huge dome of water, fifty to one hundred miles wide, that sweeps across a coastline where a hurricane makes land. A storm tide is a combination of a storm surge and a regular monthly high tide. When they come together, water heights are at their greatest.

In September 1900, a deadly hurricane swept over the port town of Galveston, Texas. It caused the worst storm tide in United States history. The streets were flooded to depths of fifteen feet and higher. Winds gusted to more than 100 miles per hour, ripping off roofs and uprooting trees. Huge chunks of buildings flew through the air.

Before the hurricane struck, Galveston had been a beautiful city of large homes and broad streets. After the storm it was a scene of utter destruction. The storm killed at least twelve thousand people and swept thousands of homes into the sea. Ships were left stranded and wrecked miles from their moorings. Even the shoreline had changed: It was now three hundred feet inland from where it had been before the storm. Since then, Galveston has built a seawall that has protected the city from the force of storm tides.

Hurricanes are the world's worst storms. That may seem strange, because tornadoes have stronger winds that can reach over 300 miles per hour. Hurricane winds rarely blow at even half that speed. But a tornado is usually less than a mile wide on the ground, and even a small hurricane is hundreds of miles wide.

Tornadoes usually last less than an hour, while hurricanes last days or even weeks. Every second, a large hurricane releases the energy of ten atomic bombs like those used in World War II. A hurricane can cause more damage than any other single weather event.

Hurricanes have numbers as well as names. The Saffir-Simpson Hurricane Scale is based on the strength of the hurricane's spinning winds. The weakest hurricanes are rated 1, and the strongest are rated 5. Hurricanes with a rating of 3 or higher are major hurricanes. There are only about three major hurricanes a year. But even hurricanes with a rating of 1 or 2 are very dangerous.

THE SAFFIR-SIMPSON HURRICANE SCALE

CATEGORY 1: Wind speeds of 74 to 95 miles per hour. Slight damage to trees, shrubbery, and mobile homes. Irene in 1999 was a category 1 when it hit southeast Florida.

CATEGORY 2: Winds of 96 to 110 miles per hour. Moderate damage. Some trees and mobile homes blown over. Houses damaged. Coastal roads may flood two to four hours before the eye arrives. Floyd in 1999 was a category 2 when it hit the North Carolina coast.

CATEGORY 3: Winds of 111 to 130 miles per hour. Extensive damage. Large trees blown down and mobile homes badly damaged. Small buildings damaged. Fran in 1996 was a category 3 and caused $3.2 billion of damage when it hit Cape Fear in North Carolina. It caused flooding rains up to Michagan.

CATEGORY 4: Winds of 131 to 155 miles per hour. Extreme damage. Complete destruction of mobile homes and much damage to other buildings. Hurricane Opal, which hit the Florida panhandle in 1995, was a category 4. It caused over $2 billion of damage, and fifty-nine people died.

CATEGORY 5: Winds of greater than 155 miles per hour. A catastrophe. Complete destruction of many roofs, doors, and windows. Major flooding. Camille in 1969 was a category 5, with winds as high as 200 miles per hour. About two hundred fifty people died because of high winds and flooding in Mississippi, Louisiana, and Virginia.

The strength of a hurricane depends upon how fast the winds spin around the eye of the storm. Hurricanes spin something like ice skaters. When skaters spin with outstretched arms, the spin is slow and skaters may be wobbly and unsteady. But when skaters tuck their arms in tightly, they spin faster and faster and are sharply upright. The tighter a hurricane is packed together, the faster are its winds.

Hurricane-force winds rip pieces off roofs, tear the siding off houses, and carry off toys, building materials, and other items left outside. These become missiles during a hurricane, dangerous to people as well as to property. Category 4 Hurricane Hugo in 1989 battered Charlotte, North Carolina—about 175 miles inland—with 100-mile-per-hour winds that knocked down trees and power lines.

Hurricanes also produce tornadoes. Tornadoes most often start in the bands of thunderstorms well away from the eye of the hurricane. But sometimes tornadoes are produced near the eye wall. Tornadoes produced by hurricanes are usually weaker than regular tornadoes and last only a few minutes. Some hurricanes set off dozens of small tornadoes.

Hurricanes are deadly, not just because of their winds, but also because they produce such heavy rains. The rains cause flooding along the coastline and even well inland, hundreds of miles from the coast. Torrential rains also trigger landslides and mudslides, particularly in hilly or mountainous areas. Flash floods happen without warning in low-lying areas. Flooding along the banks of rivers and streams can last several days after the storm.

The amount of rainfall during a hurricane is not related to the force of the spinning winds but rather to the speed of the storm. Slow-moving hurricanes produce more rainfall and can cause more damage from flooding than faster-moving, more powerful storms.

Hurricane Floyd, which struck in September 1999, was a slow-moving hurricane that produced tremendous rainfall in the eastern United States. Many states became disaster areas. More than fifty people died from inland flooding caused by the rains, including thirty-five in North Carolina.

The worst hurricane in the United States in terms of property damage was Hurricane Andrew. Andrew became a tropical storm in the southern Atlantic Ocean on August 17, 1992. At first, Andrew was a small storm with winds of about 40 miles per hour. But the storm rapidly gained strength over the warm waters, and wind speeds reached 155 miles per hour. Andrew was a category 5 hurricane by the time it passed over the Bahamas and began heading east toward Florida.

Andrew hit the coastline of southern Florida on August 24. It was moving quickly and dropped about seven inches of rain across the state. Even more rain would have fallen had it been moving slowly. Storm tides reached seventeen feet along Biscayne Bay.

Wind speeds started to decrease over land, but Andrew quickly reached the warm waters in the Gulf of Mexico, where it regained 120-mile-per-hour winds. Then Andrew turned and slammed into the shoreline of Louisiana on August 26.

Andrew left a path of destruction in its wake. Damages totaled more than $25 billion. Thousands of people had lost their homes. More than a million people had been evacuated. But fewer than fifty-five people died, because of early hurricane warnings.

eather forecasters at the National Hurricane Center were able to give a twenty-one-hour advance warning of Hurricane Andrew. This made it possible for people to flee dangerous low-lying places along the coast and go to safer spots inland.

Forecasters need to find where a hurricane is developing and how strong it is. At one time this was possible only when people saw the storm from a ship or from land. Nowadays forecasters use satellite images, airplanes, radar, and computers to track a hurricane.

Weather satellites orbit the earth at an altitude of nearly twenty-two thousand miles over the equator. The satellites send back images day and night of bands of clouds and early signs of a tropical storm. To get accurate readings of wind speed and pressure, pilots and scientists fly right through a hurricane into its eye.

When a hurricane gets close to the coast, it is pictured on land-based weather radars. Doppler radars show wind speeds and location and quickly detect changes. The National Hurricane Center takes the information from radars and other sources and uses computers to help forecast the path, speed, and strength of hurricanes.

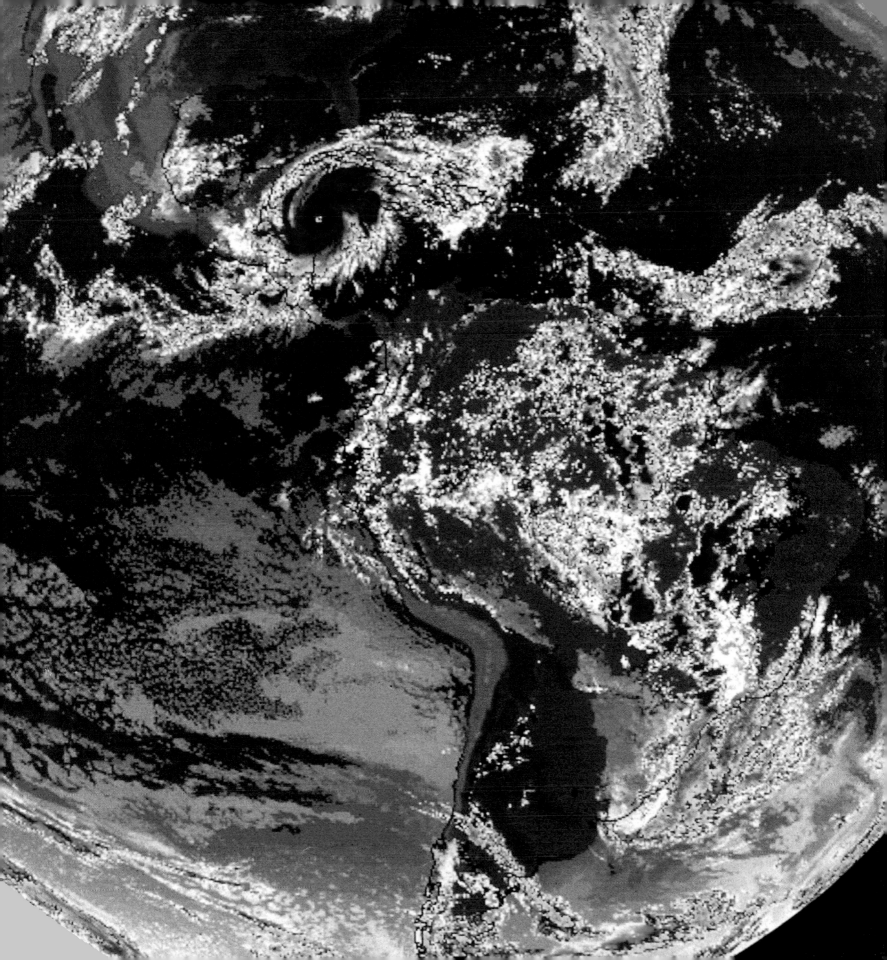

Hurricane and storm warnings are broadcast over radio and television and are also available on the Internet. National Oceanic and Atmospheric Administration (NOAA) Weather Radio broadcasts warnings, watches, forecasts, and other weather information twenty-four hours a day. These radio stations cover all the states, coastal waters, Puerto Rico, and United States Pacific territories.

A hurricane or a flood *watch* is usually given within thirty-six hours of an approaching storm. During a watch, it's important to prepare and decide what you and your family are going to do during the storm. A hurricane or a flood *warning* is usually given within twenty-four hours for a particular area. During a warning, listen to local radio or television stations for safety instructions.

National Weather Service (NWS) radios are specially equipped to give you immediate news about tropical hurricanes and floods. Regular NWS programs send out a special tone that turns on these radios in the listening area when there is an emergency. The radios can be connected to lights, computers, even bed shakers so that everyone can get the information. Details about NWS radios can be found at www.nws.noaa.gov/nwr on the Internet.

Because of early warnings, the number of hurricane-related deaths has decreased in the United States in recent years. But hurricanes still remain a danger along the Atlantic coast and the Gulf of Mexico.

Scientists think that, potentially, the most dangerous place in the United States during a hurricane is New Orleans. That's because a storm surge could cover the low-lying city with twenty feet of water. Southwest Florida from Tampa Bay to the Everglades National Park is also dangerous, because the area is also very close to sea level.

If you are ever caught in a hurricane, it's important to know what to do. The first thing to remember is to listen closely to the radio, television, or NOAA Weather Radio for official bulletins. Follow instructions and leave immediately with your family if told to do so.

Only stay in a house if you are not ordered to leave. Stay away from windows and doors during the storm. During the worst of the storm, lie on the floor under a table or another sturdy object. Make sure you have a battery-driven portable radio and keep listening for storm information. Keep on hand at least a three-day supply of water and food that won't spoil.

Even after a hurricane passes by, conditions outside may still be dangerous. Here are some tips for you and your family.

- Keep listening to the radio or television for updates on flooding and highway conditions. Wait until an area is declared safe before going back into it.

- Stay away from moving water. Rapidly moving water even less than a foot deep can sweep you away. If you see water flowing across a street, turn around and go another way.

- Don't play in flooded areas. They are dangerous. The water may also be electrically charged from downed or underground power lines.

- Use a flashlight for emergency lighting. Don't use a candle or a flame indoors if the power goes off.

- Use bottled or stored water for drinking and cooking. Use tap water only when local officials say it is safe.

- Use the telephone only for emergency calls. If someone needs to be rescued or helped, call the police or local officials.

By preparing ahead and listening to the radio and following instructions, everyone can be much safer during a hurricane.

People are now much more aware of hurricanes than they were twenty-five years ago. When a hurricane threatens the United States, it becomes big news on television and radio. Even people who live in the middle of the country and will never experience a hurricane at home are interested in what's happening during the storm.

Along the East Coast, hurricanes are a fact of life. But nowadays forecasts, combined with timely warnings about hurricane dangers, are saving lives. The more we learn about hurricanes, the better our chances of coming through them safely.